PUT YOUR BIG BOY PANTS ON

How To Master Your Mind And Emotions
Build Superior Mental Toughness
Think Positive And Live The Good Life

MARK LLEWHELLIN

Book 9 in the
Mark Llewhellin
Success and Happiness Series

DEDICATION

This book is dedicated to the love of my life, my little miracle, Léon James Llewhellin, who I love more than anyone in the world. You are kind, thoughtful, well balanced and you are already achieving great things in your life.

Words cannot describe how much I love you and how proud I am of the person you are.

To you the reader. When times are tough… put your big boy pants on!

GET TWO OF MARK'S BOOKS FOR FREE

Join Mark's team for information on new books along with special offers and pick up a FREE copy of Mark's 5 star reviewed books:

'The Underdog' and 'Delusions Of Grandeur.'

Details can be found at the end of this book.

"Our greatest glory is not in never falling, but in rising every time we fall."

– Confucius

TABLE OF CONTENTS

INTRODUCTION

"What you're supposed to do when you don't like a thing is change it. If you can't change it, change the way you think about it. Don't complain."

– Maya Angelou

A few months before publishing this book I was talking to a friend. She's in her 30s and had been married for many years with three beautiful children. She and her husband ran a successful business, the children were healthy and life was good.

Then one day, out of the blue, they both got terrible news. Her husband was diagnosed with an aggressive form of cancer. One minute they lived an idyllic life and the next minute their universe was thrown upside down.

Her husband, a mentally strong, salt-of-the-earth-type person, was determined to beat the cancer for himself and his beautiful family. He had everything to live for! After the diagnosis there was not one moment to lose and chemotherapy along with other treatment started almost immediately. Her husband fought as hard as he could.

Nine months after first being diagnosed, he lost his battle and died!

The man she adored was gone. This beautiful, kind-hearted wife and mother was heartbroken and now left to bring up her three grieving children.

Several months after my friend's husband had passed, I offered her one of my books. She chose 'Man The F*ck Up.'

Knowing what she'd been through, I said to her, "Not all the information in the book is as harsh as the title."

She paused for a second and said, "I hope it is. I need some straight talking to lift me and motivate me."

After she read 'Man The F*ck Up' she messaged me and said, "Book read… wow!"

When you put a book out into the world, you never know how somebody is going to react to it. All I can do is publish books I love, and I believe in. Fortunately, my friend loved the book. It has helped her put things into perspective and to stay strong for herself and her family during these challenging times.

'Put Your Big Boy Pants On' is similar because it doesn't pull any punches. There is no mollycoddling in this book. The harsh truth is people who are mollycoddled get brutalised by life!

When life beats the shit out of you, you've got to get tough and you've got to come out punching. You can't just sit in the corner and cry about it for the next 5, 10 or 20 years. If you do, you will not only ruin your own life, but you will be like a dark cloud to people around you.

You've got to ask yourself two very simple questions. Do I want to be

1. a dark cloud that pulls people down

or

2. a ray of sunshine that lifts people up?

If you care about your family and friends, then you need to choose option two!

You may have read other books in my 'Success and Happiness Series.' If you have, you'll know I write about winners. Not just in terms of how the world views their success, but people who have overcome their own personal battles in life. There's been times where they could've just thrown the towel in. They could've just quit and thought, fuck this, it's too big a price to pay. But they didn't, they kept going.

They had doubts and fears, but they summoned the

mental strength and will power to keep grinding away until they crossed the finish line.

Your finish line might be to achieve a big goal, getting to the end of each day, or to live a happy and fulfilled life. This book will help you achieve these things!

But make no mistake, life isn't all puppy kisses, rainbows, and roasting marshmallows over a campfire on a warm summer's evening. Whether or not we like it, there will be times in our lives when one thing after the other will go wrong. There will be times when you will be caught underneath a thunderstorm of faeces.

'The Universe,' 'Life,' 'God,' 'The Devil,' 'Fate,' or whatever you want to call it, will try to mess with your head and break you!

And no matter how many times you try to avoid the setbacks and heartache, life will come for you like serial killer Michael Myers out of the Halloween movies. Just when you think you've escaped with your life, it will come around the corner and try to fuck you up again!

Life can be relentless in its quest to bring you to your knees.

If you've seen the 'Taken' movie, you'll be aware of Liam

Neeson's famous speech that he gives to his daughter's kidnapper.

It's similar to life. It's like Life is saying,

"I know who you are. I know what you want. I have a very particular set of skills, skills I have acquired since the dawn of time. Skills that make me a nightmare for people like you. There is nothing you can do to make me stop coming after you. Whether you're good or bad person, a kind or a nasty person, I will look for you, I will find you, and I will fuck you up!"

You probably don't need me to tell you that's how brutal life can be sometimes.

Life can hurt you. No matter how positive you are, or how tough you are, there will be certain points when life will smash you to the canvas. The good news is this book will help you get back up when you've been knocked down. It will help you develop more mental toughness than you've ever had!

'Put Your Big Boy Pants On' will help you master your emotions, become a stronger person, and overcome the challenges in your life.

Maybe your reasons for becoming mentally tougher are

because you want to be a stronger and more positive role model for your children. You may want more mental toughness to grow your business, become a better employee, achieve a new fitness goal, or some other aspiration.

Getting through this life in one piece will require you to wear big boy pants. It's survival of the fittest out there. The weak crumble and the strong survive!

I didn't make those rules, that's just the way life is. The good news is, when you put your big boy pants on, you'll not only inspire others, but you'll achieve far more with your life!

This book is also for the person who has been through psychological hell and wants to turn things around for the better. It will help you develop superior mental toughness so you can live the life that you deserve. And this book will help you become happier and a more fulfilled person.

Life can be tough, but you are tougher!

So let's jump in!

CHAPTER 1

THE CRY-BABY CULTURE

"We have to choose these great fucking magical words that make people feel good. Tell yourself the truth. If someone calls you fat, they may be bullying you, but you might be fat. If someone calls you dumb, it's mean, but you might be fucking dumb. It's life. Take it for what it's worth and change it."

– David Goggins

Today we live in a cry-baby culture. There's never been a time in history where so many people are complaining about trivial things. They're the ones that wear little boy pants and spit their dummies out when things don't go their way.

The crazy thing about these complainers is, 99% of them live in super rich countries and they have opportunities all around them.

One reason so many people complain is because they hear lots of other people moaning. If they hear someone complaining, they think, "Hang on a minute, I want to tell everyone about how bad I've got things." They somehow feel left out if they too are not complaining about their situation.

They harp on about the so-called injustices they have to suffer. Little do they realise, by complaining they are sapping their energy and are making themselves unhappy.

If I was the leader of an alien race and I wanted to attack Earth, now would be the time! They're probably sitting there with their big-ass green heads, thinking to themselves, "This planet is full of people wearing little boy pants."

We live in an offended culture. There's not much that people can do or say these days without someone being offended. Fortunately, there are still some tough people out there. But like the Spartans, they are a minority.

Even some of the most well-off or super-rich and super privileged are wearing little boy pants. Maybe they feel they still haven't got enough money, or maybe they feel the press are too invasive of their privacy. The irony of it is that when the media goes away, they then turn on their heel and want more attention.

They want the attention but not the criticism. They believe they should be praised most of the time and if they don't get enough adulation from people, they throw their teddy in the corner and say, "It's not fair." They forget about all of the positives in their life and focus more on the negatives.

However, you don't need to be rich and famous to be lucky. If you're living in a developed country, you're already living a privileged life.

It doesn't matter what your race, gender, colour of your skin, or your religion, your opportunities are phenomenal compared to billions of people around the world! There are now millions of successful people, no matter what race, gender, colour, or backgrounds.

In the UK, we're lucky to have the NHS (National Health Service), whereas many countries have to pay insurance to receive medical treatment. And if they haven't got the money, it can be an extremely stressful time for them. Billions of people living in third world countries are in a far more challenging situation because they have no access to medication and life-saving medicines are often out of reach.

Imagine how frustrating it would be if one of your loved ones died because you had no access to medicine and you know hundreds of millions of people in the rich countries take that medicine for granted. To us in the western world, it's just a trip down to the doctors.

More people die from diarrhoea each year than from suicide, homicide, wars, and terrorism combined. One third of the people who die from diarrhoea are children under five years old.

It's so important to focus on our blessings! When things go wrong, chances are most of the time we'll be able to do something about it and create a better outcome.

When I joined the army and I wanted to be a commando, I had to put my big boy pants on and go for it. My fitness back then was a bag of shit. But rather than feel I was at a disadvantage compared to my friends, I trained my ass off, passed the course and went on to complete far tougher physical challenges.

I could've just bitched about why it wasn't fair because so many people were a lot fitter than me naturally. I could've complained that I didn't receive a large inheritance and said how unfair life was to me compared to others. Some people didn't have to work as hard as I did on their fitness. And some people were given greater advantages financially than me and you.

So what?

Now is not the time to complain, now is the time to focus on what you want out of life, put your big boy pants on and move forward! Maybe you think life has given you a bum deal. Maybe you're dragging up past events and feeling sorry for yourself. Maybe you keep on replaying decisions you've made that you've later regretted.

If you feel sorry for yourself or find yourself complaining to others, it's time to let that shit go!

It's time to feel grateful for what you've got, put your big boy pants on, and move forward!

CHAPTER 2

SHARP THINKING

"If you want to be successful, then you have to have drive and you don't give up."

– Roald Dahl

In the 19th century, a travelling salesman went around knocking on doors trying to sell bottle caps.

Most of the individuals he met liked him and he was easy to get along with, but he wasn't a massive fan of being rejected on doorsteps. His dream was to invent and improve things rather than knocking on people's doors all day.

He tried many things in life but couldn't seem to make a success of himself financially. At 40 years old, he moved back in with his parents because he couldn't afford a mortgage and couldn't afford to pay rent.

The young salesman was struggling to make a living. He had doubts he would ever live up to his parent's expectations and become a success. But no matter how hard things were for him, he got up every day, put his big boy pants on, and did the best he could with the time he was given each day.

Many people looked down at him because of the type of job he did. Even though he knew he was bringing money in by selling bottle caps, he wanted something more in life.

He admired his boss, who was a guy by the name of William Painter. Painter was the inventor of the disposable bottle cap that his employees were selling. Painter's idea earlier on in life was to keep inventing things until one of them become a big success, which he found with his disposable bottle caps.

One day Painter gave the young salesman a bit of advice. Painter advised his employee that he should invent a product that can only be used once. That way, once the product is used, the customer becomes a repeat customer because they need the product again.

The young salesman was confused because he thought the key to success was to build something that would last. However, although that may be true with some products, it isn't true for everything.

Back in the old days, the cut-throat razor, like the type you'd see in a cowboy movie, were the 'in thing'.

One morning, while the young salesman was shaving, he cut himself with his cut-throat razor. It was at that point he got an idea.

There were many problems associated with a straight razor a.k.a. the cut-throat razor.

The first problem was that, if it cut you, it could cut you deeply. But it wasn't just getting cut that was dangerous. In the 1800s there was also a much greater risk of infection. Some individuals even died from the infection they got while cutting themselves shaving. Back then, penicillin simply didn't exist.

The other problem with this type of razor was it always needed sharpening, and it was often the blunt blades that cut people while shaving.

The young man used his imagination and thought to himself,

"What if a blade could be created that didn't need sharpening and could be thrown away after you used it once?"

Times were tough for the young salesman but he didn't just come up with the idea and do nothing. He put his big boy pants on and took action, massive action!

The young salesman conducted lots of experiments and

used sheet steel for his choice of blade. Sheet steel was the only metal cheap enough to buy where you wouldn't mind throwing it away when you finished with it. Unfortunately, sheet steel was too soft and couldn't keep a sharp edge.

After six months of trying to develop a razor, the salesman (and now inventor) was getting frustrated by working on his own. He then decided he needed other people to help him make his dream become a reality.

The young salesman found different experts, and they all told him that sheet steel was useless. They said it couldn't hold a sharp edge and it couldn't be sharpened because it was too thin and would buckle.

Nevertheless, he kept on trying to make it work but was failing again and again. However, even after all his failures, he never quit. He put his big boy pants on every day and believed that he could become successful if he just kept going.

Then, one day, he met a man called William Nickerson. Nickerson had a reputation for achieving things that many people couldn't. However, after lots of failures, Nickerson found the experts were right… sheet steel alone simply would not work. When they realised this, they knew they had to change something, so they came up with the idea to put the sheet steel in between two other metals to strengthen it.

They decided that iron would provide strength on the outside and then put sheets of copper to conduct heat next to the iron for forging the metals. In the middle of the iron and copper, they would put sheet steel for the blade. They could now forge the metals and could produce a blade that was strong enough and sharp enough.

It would also be cheap enough for people to dispose of and buy new ones without it costing much.

In his first year of trading, he sold 51 razors and 168 blades. Not a massive amount, and certainly not enough to make a good living. However, he believed in himself and in his product. Rather than give up after the first year, he put his big boy pants on and tried again the next year.

The salesman was brilliant with his marketing and got celebrity endorsements for his razor blades. He wasn't just trying to sell a product; he was trying to sell the idea of how men could become powerful and attractive just like the celebrity sportsmen that were endorsing his razors.

In year two, he sold 90,888 razors and over 120,000 blades. By the time he was 55, he dominated the razor and razor-blade market!

The United States government supplied all their troops in World War 1 with his razors. This was because he convinced the government it would give soldiers a close shave, resulting in a tighter fitting gas mask so they were less likely to be killed from a gas attack.

Although there were several models of the safety razor by other people, no one could produce a blade like his in the early days. The salesman helped millions of people in their day-to-day lives and created the biggest razor company in the world.

His name? 'King Camp Gillette.'

Today over 600 million disposable razors are used every day, It's a $34 billion-year global market!

However, the Gillette company didn't rest on their laurels in the early days when they were the top company. They are constantly trying to improve their razors and stay ahead of the competition. In the Reading innovation centre, Gillette has established a building to understand the way people shave. Roughly 120 biologists, pharmacists, chemists and aeronautical engineers work there for the research and development of safety razors.

Every morning there can be up to 80 volunteers that go into the building and start shaving as part of an experiment to make the razors better. Gillette analyses the blade and the grip of the razor and is constantly researching on how to make a better razor. They spent over $700 million in research and development costs from 1998 for the Mac 3 and the Gillette Fusion series.

Gillette continue to pump out new products and are Masters of Marketing! They know that if they don't continuously try to improve their product and keep on advertising, their competitors will take over. Everything that Gillette does is on the cutting edge (excuse the pun) of technology.

At the time of writing, Gillette has roughly 60% of the market. Wilkinson Sword has 18% and brands like BIC and King of Shaves have most of the rest of the market.

Here are some of the key points we can learn from the Gillette story:

- Think big.
- Listen to successful people.
- Ask yourself questions.
- Be easy to get along with.

- Take risks.
- Be willing to experiment.
- The experts aren't always right.
- Failing in something can lead you on to something greater.
- Always look to improve things.
- Form partnerships with successful people.
- Think outside of the box.
- Use your imagination.
- Get other people to help you make your dream come true.
- Believe in your dream.
- Don't give up.
- Believe in yourself.

CHAPTER 3

BADASS BADGER MINDSET

"I love those who can smile in trouble, who can gather strength from distress, and grow brave by reflection. 'Tis the business of little minds to shrink, but they whose heart is firm, will pursue their principles unto death."

– Leonardo da Vinci

When we think of fearless animals, we usually think of animals such as lions, hippos, or crocodiles.

However, there is one little critter in the animal kingdom that trumps these bad boy animals for pure bravery.

Out of all the animals in the world, there is one that claims the title of the most badass!

Even though it's small, it wears some of the biggest big boy pants in the animal kingdom! It gives no fucks for anyone or anything. And Guinness World Records recognises it as 'The World's Most Fearless Animal.'

Enter 'The Honey Badger!'

The honey badger is a mammal that lives in Africa, the Indian subcontinent, and south-west Asia.

However, it isn't a badger. It's basically a skunk/polecat-looking animal on steroids.

It's only the size of a small dog but when it faces deadly creatures, it doesn't give two fucks and will fight them!

Honey badgers stay with their mum for the first 12 months of their life and are taught valuable life lessons. The number one lesson is finding food!

The honey badger isn't a very efficient hunter in its early years. However, just as humans aren't experts when they start something new, the honey badger gets better at getting what it wants with more experience.

The honey badger spends most of its time on its own, and that's how it likes to roll. When it needs food, the honey badger doesn't have it easy like most humans, where we must work for our food.

In sub-Saharan Africa, snakes kill around 30,000 people a year. But the honey badger couldn't give two fucks about snakes. It puts his big boy pants on and climbs trees to kill deadly cobras. It also eats venomous scorpions.

Honey badgers, as the name suggests, love honey. African bees can be deadly, but the honey badger gives no fucks when it wants something to eat.

A honey badger isn't just fearless, it can also take a lot of pain. The honey badger can get hundreds of painful bee stings, but it never gives up and is relentless in its quest to get honey.

In the National Geographic documentary, 'The Legendary Honey Badger,' the honey badger takes on a puff adder. While trying to kill the snake, the honey badger gets bit on the cheek but soon sends the venomous viper to snake heaven.

Honey badgers have an incredibly strong immune system. While bites from cobras and adders can kill most animals, the venom just sends the honey badger to sleep for a couple of hours. When the honey badger wakes up, it's fresher than a cool breeze on a warm summer's day and just goes about its business.

If a bigger predator such as a hyena or a lion comes near the honey badger, the honey badger ferociously snaps at the animal and can also squirt a nasty-smelling fluid from its sphincter. When a honey badger gets into a conflict with a hyena, the honey badger goes underneath the hyena and bites it on the back of the legs. This usually ends up with a hyena giving in and running away.

It has incredible strength and stamina for its size. It's not only a fearless little critter, but it also has a tremendous amount of endurance and can walk up to 20 miles a night looking for food.

A honey badger's major goal is to get food. It's a survivor and doesn't care how it gets food. It's just as happy being a scavenger in rubbish dumps as it is hunting for food.

In the documentary 'Honey Badgers: Masters of Mayhem,' animal sanctuary owner Brian Jones rescued a honey badger by the name of Stoffel who was about to get killed by a local farmer. The farmer threatened to kill Stoffel because he was eating and destroying anything in his path on the farmer's land.

When Brian took Stoffel in, he found out that Stoffel would attack anything no matter how big. He even grabbed a fully-grown rhinoceros from underneath and wouldn't let go. It's like a three-year-old toddler taking on the 6ft 9inch world heavyweight champion, Tyson Fury.

How many animals do you know that will dig under an electric fence to get into a lion enclosure? The honey badger does!

When the lions approached Stoffel, he knew he couldn't beat them because of his size, so he went for their nut sack! At one stage Stoffel was chasing a lion. However, the lion turned around and grabbed Stoffel in its mouth. But because the honey badger has fairly loose skin, Stoffel pivoted and bit the lion, drawing blood from the lion's face.

Unfortunately, round two didn't go so well for Stoffel. The lions nailed him and put him in the animal hospital for two months. Although honey badgers are fearless, they can occasionally be killed by big cats.

However, after his two months in hospital, Stoffel got back up and went about his day as fearless as ever.

Honey badgers are not only brave, but they are also great problem-solvers and have exceptionally large brains in ratio to their size. This means that when in an enclosure they can slide bolts across to open gates.

When Brian built a wall enclosure, Stoffel would climb up the trees in the enclosure and jump out. After the trees were cut down, Stoffel would move the branches to the corner of the wall, then climb up the branches and out of the enclosure.

When all the branches were taken out of the enclosure. Stoffel pushed the rocks in the enclosure to the corner of the wall and climbed up the rocks and over the wall. When all the rocks were taken out of the enclosure, Stoffel still didn't give up. He put his big boy pants on and dug up a mud pile. He then put the mud pile next to the wall and climbed on the mud pile, enabling him to climb over the wall.

No matter what the situation, the honey badger always wants to win. It thinks its way to success and bravely charges forward to get what it wants in life.

That's what we need in life. We need a badass honey badger mindset!

The honey badger knows it must eat to survive. If it could go out each morning and easily get its food, that would be great. However, that's not the way things are. Sometimes the honey badger must fight for a meal.

To get through this life and achieve your goals, you don't need to take on snakes, scorpions or killer bees. You don't need to fight a rhinoceros or walk into a lion enclosure to prove yourself. Neither do you need to squirt nasty substances from your anal passage. That one is optional.

However, what you will need to do is bravely go after what you want in life!

Defend what you have and no matter what the odds, take on the enormous challenges. When a honey badger gets bitten by a snake, mauled by a lion or anything else, it doesn't sit there in the corner and feel sorry for itself.

Fuck that! The honey badger put his big boy pants on, gets back up, takes massive action, and moves forward with its life.

When you put your big boy pants on and take some risks, just like the honey badger, you may get mauled. Not necessarily physically, but mentally beaten up. And when you take on big goals, things may not always go your way.

However, if you keep the honey badger mentality of getting back out there and boldly going for what you want, your life will be much richer in every way.

So put your big boy pants on, take on big challenges, and never give in!

CHAPTER 4

POSITIVE INTERPRETATION

"People are not disturbed by things, but by the view they take of them."
– Epictetus

While writing this book, I noticed a one-star review of my book 'Rhino Skin.' The overwhelming majority of my reviews are five-star, so to get a one-star view was weird.

This reviewer 'Johnny,' complained the book had stories about people who never cared about anybody and just kept going.

These so-called people who don't care about anyone included 'The Indian Dalit women' who became the best drummers in a once male-dominated event. These women inspired and helped oppressed third-world women by showing them they too can achieve great things in their own lives.

However, Johnny thought little of these women.

'Rhino Skin' also told the story of Michael Faraday, whose brilliance lead to inventions such as the:

- Washing machine.
- Vacuum cleaner.
- Air-conditioner.
- Refrigerator.
- Freezer.
- Laptop.

Also, trains, electric cars, and other amazing inventions I listed in 'Rhino Skin.'

Faraday also invented the Faraday Cage – a system built into over one billion vehicles to save people from being electrocuted by lightning strikes. These vehicles include cars, buses, vans, lorries, trains and aeroplanes.

But Johnny wasn't impressed!

Neither was Johnny impressed with Aneurin Bevan, who set up the NHS and has, along with the brilliant medical professionals, saved millions of people's lives.

Johnny didn't get the 'How To' information from the book. This made me chuckle because I write my books so even a nine-year-old child could understand the simplistic 'How To' content in them.

He then blabbed on about some other stuff that made little sense.

Fortunately, before my book gets published, it is first sent to my 'Advance Reader Copy (ARC) Team.'

This team of over 100 people picks up on things that aren't quite right with the early manuscript. This can be from grammar to the general content of the book. They provide valuable feedback and constructive criticism to make the book the best it can be before it is made available to the public.

As I'm writing these words, I keep chuckling to myself at Johnny's review. Johnny belongs to the cry-baby culture and wears little boy pants. He wants to read a book where all his dreams will come true by complaining and not taking any positive action.

However, when you want to change your life, you've got to change some things in your life. You can't just sit in your armchair, complain about things and wait for a winning lottery ticket that will take care of all your challenges.

Johnny is the type of person who you could give £50 million to, and he would complain that he didn't have £100 million. There are some people that will never be satisfied. Ironically, these are the people with the worst lives. Not because of what's happened to them, but because of how they think. It's their own internal dialogue that is putting the brakes on their own life.

Some authors would be devastated by a review like this. They let keyboard warriors negatively affect their day. A review like that could break some authors and stop them from writing any more books.

However, the review had a positive effect on me. First, because I knew he didn't know what he was talking about. And secondly because he gave me more real-life material to write about in this book. Of course, we'll never be friends, send each other Christmas cards or go on holidays together, but I think I can live with that.

I simply don't have time to write negative reviews. It makes me look weak, and it sets a terrible example for my son. However, if I do like something, I leave a review because I feel grateful for what I received, and I want other people to benefit.

The last review I wrote was about a pair of cowboy boots I received. Not that I go around the UK riding bulls or lassoing stray dogs. Heck, I just like the boots.

My review went something like this:

"My god these boots are epic! The company did a great job with the speedy delivery, and the quality of the boots is outstanding. They look incredible. I don't know whether to wear them, or put them on the mantelpiece and just admire them. And the smell? Ahhhhh, that beautiful new leather smell. I love it! I can't wait to strut around in these new bad boys!"

How do you think writing that review made me feel? Pretty damn good! I also know when the owner or employees of the company read that review, they're also going to feel pretty good about their product and the service they're providing.

It's a win-win for everyone!

The sad thing for Johnny is, he'll probably go through the rest of his life complaining and feeling hard done by. And for these very reasons, he will never achieve much. He'll always blame people for everything, and he'll never feel happy in life.

When you come across similar situations, just know that it's the other person who has lost out, not you. And when you are criticised, think about how you can mentally turn that criticism to your advantage just like I did.

The person who always looks for the positive in things is always going to be happier than the person who complains and feels hard done by.

So, when someone fires a shot across your bows, take the higher ground. Put your big boy pants on and merrily move forward with a smile on your face and a skip in your step.

CHAPTER 5

AGE IS NO EXCUSE

"Age is something that doesn't matter…
Unless you are a cheese."
– Billy Burke

Very often people will talk themselves out of their dreams because they say they're too young, or they are too old to do it. Although there are valid points with this statement, it doesn't apply to everyone; in fact, it applies to fewer people than we normally believe.

Yes, if you want to become the hundred metres world record holder at age 93, that's not going to be a realistic goal. It's also unlikely that a baby of six months old will work out complicated quantum mechanics. But there are many things that have been achieved by people who are old or young. Because they've done this, it opens the possibilities to what we can achieve with our own lives, whether we are a spring chicken or whether we are mature in years.

In 1918, the Farnsworth family moved to their new farm near Rigby, Idaho. The teenage son Philo was expected to follow in his father's footsteps and become a farmer. However, Philo had little interest in farming.

Philo grew up in the days of great inventors such as Alexander Graham Bell and Thomas Edison and was inspired by them. He always had a lot of energy, and he was always trying to invent new things.

At 14, Philo discovered something in the farm attic: it was a collection of books and magazines that were filled with information on scientific advancements and inventions such as the radio. However, Philo's books also mentioned about a different type of radio that hadn't been invented; it was the type that could not only transmit sounds but also transmit pictures.

Little did he know back then, it was about to change not only his life, but the lives of billions of people around the world!

Many great inventors had already tried to invent the TV but none of them had succeeded.

According to Philo's great granddaughter, he was out ploughing the field one day with two horses. When he stopped ploughing, Philo noticed the plough lines across the field. When he looked at the lines, he thought it would be possible to slice an image into parallel rows. He then wondered if a point of light moved fast enough, it could not only create pictures but also create moving pictures.

One day Philo was looking in his science journals and thought that there was another possibility of creating a better, more practical TV. He wondered if electrons could do the job because they move back-and-forth tens of thousands of times per second. However, Philo would need to find a way to control them, which was no simple task.

Philo was so excited about inventing something that could project sound and images, he showed his idea to his science teacher and drew out a picture of what he called an 'Image Dissector.' The drawing shows light entering through a lens. The light then gets converted into electrons and the electrons then pass through a vacuum which are turned into an electronic signal. This can then be beamed out all over the world like a radio signal.

Philo's teacher was blown away that a 14-year-old could come up with these ideas and understand them properly. His teacher is reported to have said, "It just might work."

There is no sole inventor of the TV because so many inventions had to be created before the television could work. There are also many types of TV. However, Philo had one of the crucial roles to play in putting the icing on the cake for the invention of the modern television.

Even though he was only 14 years old when he started his

journey, he put his big boy pants on and thought big.

Philo Farnsworth went on to hold 300 patents and became the founder of the Farnsworth Television and Radio Corporation.

Here are some key points taken from this story:

- You can achieve great things even if your age is against you.
- Follow your own dream (if it doesn't hurt anyone and is of some benefit to people), even if your family wants you to do something else.
- Be on the lookout for information that can help you achieve your dreams.
- Study what already exists and think up new ways to improve it.
- Many people will try to help you on your path.
- Think big.
- Have the courage to believe in yourself and your dreams.

Here are a few other examples of people who have achieved great things at a young age:

Blaise Pascal began studying geometry at 12. When he was 19, he developed the hand-held calculator.

Mary Shelley published 'Frankenstein' at 20.

Wolfgang Amadeus Mozart wrote his first symphony at 8.

Romanian gymnast Nadia Comăneci became an Olympic gold medallist in 1976. She was the first ever gymnast to score a perfect 10 at an Olympic gymnastics event. She was only 14 years old.

William Pitt the Younger became Prime Minister of England at 24.

Gladys Burrell ran a marathon aged 92.

John Glenn went into space at age 77.

Teiichi Igarashi climbed Mount Fuji at age 100.

William Ivy Baldwin did a tightrope walk across a canyon in El Dorado Springs, Colorado. He was 82.

Diana Nyad swam from Cuba to Florida at age 64.

Nelson Mandela was elected President of South Africa at 75.

So, no matter how old you are, put on your big boy pants (or big girl pants) and go for your goal!

CHAPTER 6

TAKE ON BIG CHALLENGES

"The biggest risk is not taking any risk. In a world that is changing really quickly, the only strategy that is guaranteed to fail is not taking risks."

– Mark Zuckerberg

I'm going to assume because you're reading one of my books that you are like me. You are a dreamer. You have hopes and dreams for a better future for yourself. You have goals you want to achieve, and you want to live life to the full.

You don't want to miss out on living an exceptional life.

To create an exceptional life, you must put your big boy or big girl pants on and take on big challenges.

To create a fulfilling life yourself, you must stretch yourself and take on big challenges. It doesn't matter whether they are big challenges to other people, all that matters is that they are big challenges to you.

When you achieve your goals, it will help you grow mentally, and you will become a much stronger individual.

However, when you're trying to achieve something new,

there are many unexpected things that will crop up out of the blue. There are things that will happen that will try to knock you off your course. One minute things are going well and the next minute, you fall ill, and you can't be as productive as you were the day before.

Maybe you've got injured, maybe there's been an unexpected nasty bill that's arrived that's going to be difficult to pay. You could have been affected by a virus and it hit your income in a bad way.

There could be a challenge in a relationship with your partner. Maybe your partner is putting the brakes on your ambitions or is jeopardising your relationship. There could be an unexpected tragedy in your family that will take the wind out of your sails.

Maybe you aren't trying to achieve something new, maybe you're just content now. That's fine; however, one thing is for sure, there will be tough times ahead.

The reality of life is, it's going to be hard, real hard at times!

There will be times when you need to sit down and take a rest, but ultimately you must put your big boy pants on and get back out there. If not for other people, then do it for yourself!

Bad things will happen that you never expected. When they do, it's time to put on your big boy pants!

In the Amazon Prime series 'Undercover Billionaire', three wealthy individuals take on a challenge where they are put in a town they are not familiar with. They don't know anyone, and they are given an old truck and $100 to survive. Their goal is to create a $1 million business within the space of 90 days.

All the wealthy individuals believed they would pull it off. However, after a few days, they were all struggling mentally. They soon realised how difficult it was when you haven't got any contacts and you have little money.

However, these individuals are winners in the game of life. They are ambitious and they are go-getters in every sense of the word.

The documentary shows them going through the mentally challenging times. It shows the doubt and insecurity they feel when things weren't going their way. Most people would've given up, but to their credit, they kept on going.

One thing they all did was they asked other people for help. They knew that without the help of other people, the goal of creating $1 million business in 90 days would be dead in the water!

They were always thinking about solutions. That's what life is. It's about finding solutions, solutions, solutions!

They had doubts, they had fears and every one of them doubted their ability to pull this challenge off at certain points.

You could argue that it's not real life and they could've gone back to their wealthy lifestyle at any time. If they had done this, then they would've looked silly on camera and it would be something they would find hard to live down.

However, the challenge was very real and even though they all struggled, they hit their target to create a $1 million business with the help of other people.

Here are some characters traits of all the wealthy people on undercover billionaire.

They

1. Told themselves they had what it takes.

2. Were willing to take big risks.

3. Set goals.

4. Visualised themselves succeeding.

5. Asked for help.

6. Risked looking a fool.

7. Put in a tremendous amount of work.

8. All experienced unexpected setbacks.

9. Picked themselves back up when times were tough.

10. Were relentless and never gave in.

If you want to grow mentally and achieve great things, then you're going to need to put on your big boy pants! It's one thing putting on your big boy pants at the start, but it's another thing keeping your big boy pants on when you experience failures and heartache.

Putting your big boy or big girl pants on isn't a one-off thing – you must put them on every single day and keep fighting!

CHAPTER 7

A MIGHTY ERECTION

"If you have built castles in the air, your work need not be lost, that is where they should be. Now put the foundations under them."

– Henry David Thoreau

At the time of writing, the Burj Khalifa is the tallest building in the world. It stands at just under 830 metres and is one of the greatest achievements in engineering history!

Before the Burj was erected, all that existed in its place was a desert.

The Burj was ground-breaking and the people that were working on the Burj had to have their big boy pants on.

Whether it was wealthy investors risking their finances, or construction workers working hundreds of metres up, it took a lot of courage to build the Burj.

When the Burj was under construction, there was an enormous sign next to it that said:

Requirements to work on this project...

1. BIG BOY PANTS

2. BIG BOY PANTS

and

3. BIG BOY PANTS

I'm joking, it didn't really have that sign - but there should have been one!

Work started on the $1.25 billion tower before the architects finished all the final plans.

Construction manager David Bradford said, "The way you have to build a building like this is you have to fast track it, so you can't wait until you get all the design in place. If you do, you'll be sitting there in your office for 3 years trying to get the design finished before you can tender it."

So how did they build such a tall building?

The fastest way to build a vast tower is with reinforced concrete using a process called 'jump-forming'.

The builders make a mould at the base of the tower.

Then, after putting in steel reinforcement bars, they pour in concrete. 12 hours later, when the concrete becomes solid, the builders lift the mould and use it to do the next level.

After they've put the steel reinforcement bars in and poured the concrete for the next level, they start again on the next level up, using the mould.

The Burj Khalifa grew at one floor a week. Later, it would grow a new floor every three days!

The team used concrete that had never been produced before and because of the high temperatures in Dubai, it was a massive challenge. Their solution to getting the concrete up to the higher floors was to pump it up with pipes.

If the concrete was too thin, it would take longer to set and cause delays. If the concrete was too thick, it could block the pipes it was being pumped up by. Also, if the concrete was too hot, it would set too quickly, and it couldn't be placed.

The engineers had to put ice and chilled water into the concrete. They would pour it at night using three of the world's most powerful concrete pumps.

The pumps delivered over 165,000 m^3 of concrete, which is enough concrete for a pavement (sidewalk) over 800 km long.

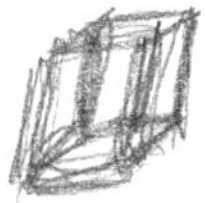

The 508 metre Taipei 101 in Taiwan was previously the world's tallest building, so architects, engineers, builders, and owners of the Burj were determined to beat the 508-metre mark.

One of the big questions was, were the foundations going to be strong enough to hold the mighty erection up?

When engineers analysed the ground under the proposed site, they found a big problem!

The top layer was 3–4 metres of sand, then below that, it was weak sandstone and limestone, which weren't good for building a foundation.

Ideally, the best type of foundation would be like hard granite that can be found in New York City.

To combat this challenge, the engineers came up with an ingenious idea based on science. They used a method of putting piles into the ground. There are two methods of piling, one of which is end-bearing piles. This is where you put the pile into the ground to rest on hard rock that can hold up the load.

The other method is the one they used. This method uses skin friction piles where the weight of the tower is carried on the friction at the side of the pile. So, the foundations rely on the firm grip created from the ground and each pile.

The engineers drove 192 piles 50 metres beneath the tower to support a raft of concrete that would be placed on top of the piles. These piles would have to hold up a phenomenal 500,000 tonnes!

To do this job the team used three of the biggest cranes in the world, which all weigh around 120 tonnes each.

For the building to reach its final height, the team had to put a spire on the top, but this was no ordinary spire. It is a 136 m tall steel pipe weighing over 350 tonnes.

However, there was a tremendous problem because they needed to lift the spire and place it on top of the building. The team couldn't get a crane up high enough to set the spire, and there is no helicopter on the planet that can lift 350 tonnes of steel.

The only way to get the spire up to the top was to assemble it in pieces inside the building and put it up piece by piece.

The Burj has over 30,000 glass panels, which is enough to cover seven football fields.

Without a way of cooling the rooms inside, it would become one massive greenhouse. This would make working and living in the Burj extremely challenging.

The solution was to have glass on the outside that reflects the heat from the sun. It does this by having a coat of thin metal on it. This gets rid of the ultraviolet radiation which would otherwise heat the tower.

Along with air-conditioning, these glass panels protect people and keep them in comfortable conditions inside the building.

One of the other challenges that the architects and engineers had was at that sort of height, the building would be exposed to high winds.

And with the building being made of steel, high winds could push the building which would mean the building would sway back and forwards and the people inside the building would experience a similar motion to being rocked back and forth on a ship.

Naturally, the last thing that people wanted was to get seasick while they were in the building!

When the Burj was being built, the engineers decided it would be better to shift the steel framework from the inside of the building to the outside of the building.

This would create an exoskeleton, so it was a lot harder for the wind to bend the building.

But because the Burj was so tall, even putting the steel on the outside wouldn't be enough.

Their solution?

They designed a tower to deflect the wind and be as aerodynamic as possible. It has also gone through extensive engineering tests to make it stand up to earthquakes.

In January 2010, the Burj Khalifa opened its doors to the public.

As well as holding the world record for the tallest building in the world, it also holds six other world records. It

- Has the tallest serviced elevator in the world.
- Is the tallest freestanding structure in the world.

- Boasts the highest outdoor observation deck in the world.
- Has the highest numbers of storeys in the world.
- Boasts the highest occupied floor in the world.

Here are some interesting facts about the Burj Khalifa.

- The Burj Khalifa is home to 900 luxury residences. These include studios, one, two, three and four-bedroom apartments and a giant five-bedroom penthouse.
- It also has 78 rooms and 82 suites for guests.
- Its prime contractor is Samsung C & T (Construction & Trading).
- Construction took 22 million work hours.
- Over 110,000 tonnes of concrete were used for the concrete and steel foundation.
- The Burj uses over 30,000 tonnes of steel.
- It is three times taller than the Eiffel Tower

- The Burj uses up to 36 megawatts of electricity, which is enough to power a town of 20,000 people.

- Over 380 engineers were involved in putting in the exterior cladding.

- The total aluminium weight used on the Burj Khalifa is the equivalent of five A380 aircraft.

- The Burj Khalifa is (at the time of writing) the tallest building in the world. It stands at 829.8 m (2,722ft).

- 15,000,000 gallons of water are collected every year.

- The tip of the spire of the Burj Khalifa can be seen up to 95 km away.

- At the peak of its construction approximately 12,000 people worked on the Burj Khalifa every day.

Let's look at what we can learn from building the Burj Khalifa that we can apply to our own lives:

- Have a big dream.

- Get advice from experts.

- Make plans.

- Don't expect to have every little detail of the plan in place.
- Creating something big usually takes money (whether it's yours or someone else's).
- Build a solid foundation.
- Improvise as you go along.
- Enlist the help of other people.
- Think up new and creative ways to be successful.
- Don't let the conditions determine your success.
- Just because something has never been done, it doesn't mean it can't be done.
- Take action.
- Put a tremendous amount of work in to achieve your goal.
- The team that built the Burj Khalifa wore big boy pants!

CHAPTER 8

STAND YOUR GROUND

"Stand your ground. Giving up and giving in is not the way. Simply and quietly claim your right to be you."
– Neale Donald Walsch

Never let people force things on you or give in to peer pressure. Especially if you know it's bad for you in the long run.

It could be drugs, alcohol, or an entire list of things that are bad for your health or could get you in trouble with the law.

I don't do things with people, or for people, if I feel it's not the right thing to do.

They could think I am a complete asshole or think I'm not cool.

But I really don't concern myself with how others think I should live 'my life' and neither should you!

It's 'your' life and you can do whatever you want with it. When you have this mindset, it will give you a massive sense of power.

Not power like some evil tyrant, but just an inner power that makes you become your own person.

If you're in a certain environment, and people are encouraging you to take drugs, drink alcohol or whatever it is, and you don't want to, it's time to grow a pair, and just refuse to do it.

The people that try to force things on you, and try to make you into somebody you're not comfortable with being, aren't worth having around in your life!

Sometimes people feel forced to fit in with their work colleagues. For example, in Hollywood some people take certain substances just to fit in. They ass-kiss successful producers, directors, casting agents and the actors to get jobs.

One thing that has become prominent over the years is people claiming sexual harassment and saying they had to sleep with a boss or they had to sleep with somebody to further their career.

In reality, they didn't 'have to' do anything they didn't want to. They could've packed their bags and walked away.

Then 10 or 20 years later, some people try to sue the

person who they slept with, even if both parties consented to the sex at the time.

If someone has been raped, that's a different story. In that case, the attacker clearly needs to go to jail.

Like most people, I have friends that have taken different types of drugs.

As far as I'm concerned, people, and my friends can do whatever they want with their life. I don't really get involved, unless I see their life is spiralling out of control and I then tell them to sort their shit out and get a grip.

What is good for you and what is bad for you isn't rocket science. We all know what's good and what's bad for us.

When somebody tries to force something on me that I don't want to do, I stand my ground, and nothing is going to move me. Anyone that's worth his or her salt in this world, will respect you more for standing your ground and being who you are rather than some sort of puppet on a string!

If somebody won't give me a job because I won't suck up to them or take drugs, they can go and take a run! However, if you're okay with doing that, and it doesn't compromise who you are, then crack on.

Sometimes certain men (especially men that are part of a team, army, rugby, football) like to see how much you can drink when they first meet you. In the early days of the army, I used to drink alcohol that I didn't like. The main thing that we used to drink was lager. Personally, I thought it was disgusting, but I still drank it because back then I wanted to fit in.

It's the same with smoking. The primary reason people smoke obviously isn't because it's good for you. So, why do people smoke? The main reason people start smoking is because they want to fit in. That's why I started smoking when I was 15. Thankfully, it didn't last, and I soon gave it up after only a few months. If the so-called 'cool crowd' in school didn't think I fitted in or didn't like me not smoking, tough shit!

If you stand your ground and do what you want to do, different people will view you in different ways.

Some people will think you're a bit of a party pooper by not doing what everyone else does; however, some people will respect you for doing what you want to do, even if it's not what they do.

Obviously, circumstances can differ, and sometimes you'll need to be a part of a team to complete a task, even if you think there is a better way of doing things. There are no set rules here, so you're the one that must take responsibility for your actions.

I was listening to a speech by motivational speaker Les Brown once. Les was involved with a bunch of guys who went to rob a store. His friends kept on at him and tried to persuade him to go with them to rob the store. When Les refused, they said that he would have a straightforward job, and all he would have to do was drive the getaway car.

"Come on Les, it's easy money!"

Les still stood his ground and refused to go on the job. His gut told him not going was the right thing to do. He wanted bigger and better things for his life! His friends thought he was a chicken and said to him he didn't have the balls to do it.

Many men get caught up trying to be 'Mr Macho' and try to prove to other people how brave they are. I guess most of us men do that to an extent and we like some recognition, as do many women. But when it goes against our core values and we feel it's wrong, that's a different story.

Les's friends gave up on trying to persuade him and got another getaway driver. Later, when they robbed the store, their getaway driver was shot dead!

I was doing some bodyguard work in Africa once and after work we had some downtime, so we went to a hotel where there were a lot of British people. Unlike the UK, there wasn't a 'no smoking ban' inside buildings, so in the bar area you could smoke if you wanted to.

My team and I were all sitting around a table and someone who we'd just met joined us and sat next to me for a chat. I usually enjoy meeting new people and having a chat with them; however, this guy lit up his cigarette and started smoking. I'm a non-smoker and a fan of health and fitness. I didn't want to breathe in his smoke, so I got up and walked off. I didn't make an issue of it, and the smoker was perfectly in his right to start smoking in this building. But I wasn't going to sit there and inhale his smoke when I didn't have to. If I thought what he was talking about was of great value to me, I may have put up with the smoke and listened while merrily filling my lungs with smoke. But what he was saying wasn't of interest to me, so I just got up and walked off!

Many people would have just stayed there not to appear rude. I have no doubt there may have been someone on our table that thought my walking off was rude. However, I'm not here to please every single person, and neither are you. I'm not saying you should appear rude as I think that being rude and obnoxious will go against you in life.

A few years ago, I was flying into Lagos, Nigeria with my new friend and colleague Dave to do some bodyguard work. Our job was to look after diplomats and protect them from Boko Haram – a terrorist organisation in Nigeria. The last thing I read about Boko Haram was in November 2020, just two months before I write these words. Haram ruthlessly killed at least 110 farm workers. The workers were just poor people that needed a job. They were either shot, or tied up and had their throats slit.

We had to fly to Lagos first, then stay in Lagos overnight and then get a connecting flight to a place called Maiduguri in the northeast of Nigeria the following day. Dave said that he was going to show me around the bars in Lagos and said that I would be leathered (very drunk), to which I replied, "No I won't be."

"You will be!" he said with a quiet confidence.

"Nah, I won't, I'm not drinking much."

I could see a look of surprise on Dave's face. I could see that he felt a bit taken aback by this comment. Perhaps he was used to taking people out on the town and getting them wasted. But this just wasn't going to happen with me. I don't mean to put out anyone, or offend anyone; I'm just being me.

I'm the same when I go on theatre tours with my mate Mark 'Billy' Billingham. Sometimes loads of us get together after the shows and have a few drinks. If I get to the stage where I feel like I want to go to bed or I just want to chill out without a crowd of people around me, I'll duly thank people for coming to the show, say how nice it was to see them, and just clear off to my bedroom!

At first, some people found it challenging and would try to encourage me to stay out, which was kind of them, and I appreciate it. But when they got to know me better, they knew that if I wanted to go, I was just going, no matter what.

Here's another example.

One day I was at a carnival with my brother, my mum, and my son. After the carnival, we were invited back to my brother's friend's house. I didn't mind taking my mum and my son to the house, as there was a bit of a garden party, but I needed to work on my books. They asked me to join the party, which again was kind of them. However, I politely thanked them for the invitation, but declined. I said that I simply needed to work on my books in my car, as I'd got a deadline to meet. Although I didn't have a deadline to reach for an editor or publisher, I had my own deadlines! I didn't mean to be rude to anyone but I, like you, have limited time. We only have 24 hours in a day, and we need to use those 24 hours wisely!

If people perceive you as rude by not going to something they've invited you to, or if you don't do something they'd like you to do, then that's something they have to deal with.

Of course, there will be times when a friend asks a favour of you, and you may have to go the extra mile even if you don't feel like it. If you're the only one that can help them, or if they've supported you in your time of need, you should probably help them as long as it doesn't compromise who you are. Helping someone if they've helped you is often the right thing to do.

There are times in your life where you will be pulled from side to side and people will want you to do all sorts of things that you don't want to do. Most of the time it's important to still be polite to people, but you still need to stand your ground, be yourself, and remain true to yourself. If you do this, then you will live a much happier and healthier life!

CHAPTER 9

SAY GOODBYE TO YOUR COMFORT ZONE

"When you go out of your comfort zone and it works, there is nothing more satisfying."

– Kristen Wiig

Achieving your dreams isn't easy, but the more confident you are, the more likely you are to achieve your goals and dreams. Being an extremely confident person is an awesome thing, but it comes at a price.

And that price is you must leave your comfort zone.

It's like that scene out of the Lord of The Rings where the little hobbit Frodo leaves his home to save the world. He is going way out of his comfort zone and massively risking his life.

When you want to achieve a big goal, chances are, you won't have to fight disgusting looking orcs, flying monsters with bad breath and spiders the size of a van.

So hey, what have you got to lose?

Being in a comfortable place is what many people want in life, but if you want to grow in confidence and ability you've got to leave your comfort zone and take risks. You must be willing to get knocked back and fail to succeed.

Look back at your own life. I bet you can think of experiences where you had to take risks, and that risk didn't pay off. You may have felt uncomfortable and even felt embarrassed that you failed. However, what you will have done is grown mentally. Rather than focus on the things you've failed at, look back into your past and think about what you have succeeded at.

I was recently reading a personal development book by another author. He advises people to write a list down of your failures. Blow that for an idea - don't do that! While his intentions may be good, that advice is poor.

I've got a lot of friends that are extremely successful in different areas of life and I've never heard one of them say the key to their success was writing down all of their failures. Sure, they acknowledge and learn from their failures, but they move forward rapidly and don't focus on them. I haven't got time to waste by writing down the failures and neither have you. It's not productive, and it's not going to get you anywhere.

However, if you want to write a list, write a list of your successes. This will give you more belief in yourself because you can see what you have achieved in the past.

To somebody else your achievements might not look like much, but that doesn't matter. All that matters is that your achievement is important to you. If you have extreme anxiety and you find it difficult going out of the front door of your house, then going out of your house is an enormous achievement!

While writing this chapter, I found it challenging to want to work. Although I am extremely driven compared to many people, there are some days where I just don't want to put the effort in. But what I do love is the end result. And the result is me producing another book that can help people all over the world. Often, I can't wait to dig into my work but some days I just don't feel like it. However, on this day, I decided to just put my big boy pants on and push through my laziness.

Is it always comfortable trying to achieve your goals? Hell no!

But when you achieve a goal that was difficult, you will treasure it more. You look back at it and know that it wasn't easy. You'll know that you had to put in effort when some days you just didn't want to. Achieving your goals takes discipline and disciplining yourself isn't the easiest or most natural thing to do.

If you want the same confidence as you've got now, or

even less confidence, stay in your comfort zone. And if you don't want to achieve anything else with your life, stay in your comfort zone. However, if you want more confidence and success, kiss your comfort zone goodbye, and focus on the big picture!

CHAPTER 10

STOP BITCHING START DOING

"The only difference between success and failure is the ability to take action."
– Alexander Graham Bell

Most people don't want a social media news feed filled with negativity from people who continuously post about how hard their life is.

People who constantly post negative things are always focusing on everything that's wrong with their lives or what's wrong with the world.

Although there are people that want a way out of their dark mental state, there are also many people who don't want to get out of that frame of mind.

As bizarre as it sounds, there are people out there who enjoy being unhappy. They are not happy in the truest sense of the word, but they feel comfortable moaning about things, and they are far too lazy or afraid to make changes.

Change can be difficult, so it's easier for people to stay with their old thought patterns and complain. You can hear it when they talk. If you say, "How are you today," they'll reply with something like,

"Another day, same shit."

"Ah, there we go."

"Ah, here I am."

These are the people that take life for granted and are not grateful for the gift of life. They choose to focus on what they haven't got; and if you talk to them too often, they'll do their very best to make you just like them.

Many people who complain and take life for granted would soon change their tune if they were told by a doctor that they only had 7 days to live. Many of these people would cling to life.

Personally, I can't stand being around people like this and try my best to avoid them. People sometimes comment on how upbeat I am. Part of my happiness is because I stay away from doom and gloom people.

Sometimes all of us will be hit by life and will feel beaten down. I've had my fair share of challenges, but I don't focus on those things day in, day out. If I focus on the negative things, I'll soon drag myself and other people down.

Many people think that being happy has got everything to do with outside circumstances, but, ultimately, we have the power to choose what we want to think about a certain situation.

One day I went to the gym and saw one of my friends that I used to work with. I asked him how things were, and he replied, "Rubbish!"

He then told me he recently drove his car down to a remote area and took a load of pills with vodka to kill himself. Fortunately, he was sick, which got rid of the pills and prevented his death.

I told him he had so much going for him and he was doing well in many areas of his life. He had a great physique, he had more money than the average person, he drove a nice car and he had a couple of successful businesses. But none of this mattered to him.

I asked him what had brought all of this on and he told me he was lonely. He said, "What's the point of having lots of things when you've got no one to share them with."

I told him if he wanted a change his situation, he needed to ask girls out. Ask them out on social media or go on something like Tinder. He scoffed at me and said, "'I'M NOT GOING ON TINDER!"

He thought it was beneath him and he shouldn't have to go onto dating sites to find somebody.

That's all down to perspective. He was stuck up about how he was going to find somebody. I've seen this happen before when I've asked couples how they first met. Sometimes, they feel embarrassed when they tell me they first meet in a local nightclub.

However, where and how you meet somebody is completely irrelevant!

If it was a girlfriend my old friend wanted, he had to get himself out of there. It doesn't matter which avenue leads to success; what matters is you get to success, whether that's finding a partner, or succeeding in another area of your life.

If you think things should just come to you, and fall in your lap, you're going to be disappointed. Whether it's health, fitness, money, relationships or a new business, you've got to go out there and make it happen! The people that wait around for things to happen are the people that get left behind in life. Many of these people suffer from depression.

My friend focused on everything that he didn't have, and that was leading him straight to big mental health problems.

A day later, I messaged him and asked if his mum was still alive. He saw the message but didn't message me back until the next day. The next day he replied and said, "Yeah, Mum is still with me," followed by a high-five emoji with a heart.

I messaged him back and said,

"That's fantastic. I know how close your mum is to you, and I know how much she loves you. Imagine your mum got beat up by 10 men. Really badly. How would that make you feel? If you did something stupid, then the pain you would inflict on her would be 1000 times worse!"

Shortly after, I spoke to him again. I do care about him and I said that I didn't mean to sound harsh or try to upset him when I'd said what I said.

He told me that there was no need to apologise and I was speaking the truth. It helped him think about his self-destructive thoughts. And it also gave him a reason he needed to carry on.

Not only that, but he also started to focus on what he was grateful for in his life.

There's nothing wrong with him wanting a partner. However, if he wants to be with somebody, he needs to stop feeling sorry for himself, put his big boy pants on, and take action to make his goal a reality.

No matter what it is you want in life, you've got to stop feel feeling sorry for yourself; it doesn't do yourself or anyone else any good. The more you feel sorry for yourself, the more likely you are to fail.

The good news is, you can turn it all around by being grateful for what you have and take action towards your goals. Sometimes you'll hit a home run and sometimes you strike out that's just the way life is.

So, when you want to turn things around, stop bitching and start doing!

CHAPTER 11

NOT ALL DREAMS COME TRUE

"You cannot have it all. And this notion that you can have it all, you can't have it all!"

– Katharine Hepburn

I've been studying personal development, psychology, mental health and self-help books for over 25 years.

Sometimes you'll come across books that say you can have EVERYTHING you've ever wanted.

If you're like me, you probably want to achieve ALL of your dreams. The good news is you can achieve an enormous number of things. However, in reality, there are so many dreams in our heads, which is highly unlikely that they're all going to come true.

I know some personal development authors and coaches say, "If you have a dream, God put that dream in your head and God wouldn't have given you that dream without the ability to achieve it."

I love the optimism here. But in this book, I want to deal with reality, not pie in the sky stuff where you fly around on your magical unicorn every day without a care in the world.

To say that you can have, do, and achieve 'everything,' is complete bollocks.

In my 47 years on this little rock we call Earth, I've never come across one person who has achieved everything and has everything they've ever wanted. To do that, it would mean experiencing no failure or loss in life.

David Beckham is one of the biggest names in football, even though he's been retired for many years. He achieved almost everything someone could ever want to achieve in football, apart from one thing. The one thing he wanted more than anything else was to win the World Cup, but it never worked out for him.

Michael Jordan is one of the greatest sports people that has ever lived. However, when Michael crossed from basketball to baseball and attempted to conquer the baseball world, it didn't go well for him.

He did extremely well just to become a professional baseball player. However, he didn't become one of the best baseball players, he didn't win the trophies he wanted to win, and he certainly didn't achieve the sort of success he wanted to achieve.

No matter how strong his mindset, no matter how positive he was, no matter how hard he worked, and no matter how successful he had been, it just didn't work out for him.

When many people see Roger Federer kicking ass in Wimbledon, they dream of being a winner just like Roger, but Roger doesn't get everything his own way.

Floyd Mayweather retired undefeated with a 50–0 record fight wins, and he is considered one of the best boxers of all time. His nickname is Floyd 'Money' Mayweather, but he dreams of being as rich as a Bill Gates, Warren Buffett, or a Jeff Bezos.

When Ronaldo received the trophy for the world's best football player, it was a dream come true for him, but he doesn't always win every match or every trophy.

If you're a woman, you probably wouldn't be disappointed if you climbed to the dizzy media heights of Oprah Winfrey, or if you were voted 'Sexiest Woman.'

You might think how great it would be to be the leader of your country, like New Zealand Prime Minister Jacinda Ardern, who was voted by Fortune Magazine as The World's Greatest Leader in 2021.

This list can go on and on.

Maybe none of those examples are your thing, but I'm sure you have had dreams of achieving or having something and it just hasn't panned out.

Walt Disney has received more Oscars than anyone in history. He got the ball rolling with creating the most successful theme parks in the world and achieved a huge number of things. Not all of his dreams came true. Walt's dream of building Walt Disney World in Florida came true, but his dream of seeing it did not. Walt died before Disney World became a reality.

No matter who you are, no matter what level of success greatness you achieve, you will not achieve every single thing you wanted to achieve. That's the way life is, and you must put on your big boy pants or big girl panties and deal with it.

Some things will go your way and some things won't!

Yes, it makes a massive difference when you've got a positive mindset, when you've got a lot of belief in yourself, when you're persistent, when you're relentless, and you never give in. But there will be times when you come unstuck in life.

And how many of us want the people we love to die? The truth is you can't have everything.

However, just because you didn't achieve something that you wanted to achieve, it doesn't mean that your life is ruined.

I failed many, many times at lots of things in my life. But rather than focus on the failure, I choose to focus on the possibilities still out there. And rather than focus on the loss of loved ones in my life, I choose to feel grateful for the time I had with them and you can do the same.

Life is a rollercoaster and you have to take the rough with the smooth. So put your big boy pants on, be grateful, stay positive and make as many dreams come true as you can!

CHAPTER 12

SHIT THINKING, SHIT LIFE

"What we achieve inwardly will change outer reality."
– Plutarch

Several years ago, I was doing night-shift security work on a solar farm. When I finished my 12-hour shift in the early hours of the morning, another security guard relieved me of my position.

Every time I saw him in the morning, I would say to him, "How are you?"

His reply was always the same, "Another shit day, shit work, shit day!"

I must admit, it wasn't the most exciting or well-paying job I've ever done, but it wasn't hard work. I knew it wasn't my dream job and I could achieve more, but I felt grateful for the work I had. It was easy work, and it was paying the bills. I could've complained about it, but I didn't see the point of making myself feel bad. Besides, that job would be a dream job for many people around the world.

What my colleague didn't realise was, he was responsible for his shit day. Every morning he would feel hard done by. He didn't have the job that he wanted, the money he thought he should get or the lifestyle he should be living. Day after day, week after week and month after month, he would make himself feel bad because he wasn't grateful for what he had.

There's nothing wrong with wanting a different job, more money or a better lifestyle.

However, when people complain about their situation and they do nothing to change it, that's committing psychological suicide.

Some people's mind becomes like a prison to them. They think they're stuck in an unpleasant situation and there's no way out of it. In reality, it's themselves that have put walls around their mind to stop them getting out of the situation they're in.

We need to look at things with a higher state of consciousness.

Imagine you are a spiritual being, looking down at yourself, assessing the situation.

By doing this, it's easier to find solutions to your challenges.

When we become self-absorbed, we see things from a limited perspective. This limits our potential and causes a lot of problems.

If you want to live a happier, healthier life and achieve more things, ask yourself questions such as:

1. How do I get my mind to a better place?

2. How can I solve the challenges that I'm going through?

3. What action can I take to improve my situation?

4. What can I already feel grateful for?

5. What positive spin can I put on my situation?

One day I put my hand under tap-water to wash my hands. Within a second, I realised this water was extremely hot and pulled my hand out of the scalding water as fast as I could. After doing that, I put my hand under cold running water to minimise the damage of the burn.

It's easy to know when we're being physically hurt. When

we do something that causes us pain, we can do something about it to stop the pain.

People usually find solutions for eliminating physical pain far quicker than they find solutions to mental suffering.

It makes little sense to keep your hand under scalding water. Not only because of the immediate pain, but the longer you keep your hand under it, the more pain you will go through, not only in the short term but also in the long term!

What many people don't realise is they are in control of feeding their mind with self-destructive thoughts. When you keep on feeding your mind with these negative thoughts, things will not get better, they'll get worse. Not only in the short term but also in the long term. It's like keeping your hand under scalding water.

However, training your mind to be aware of negative thinking and eliminating negative thinking isn't as easy as being aware of physical pain and reacting to stop that pain.

When we become more aware of what we're saying to ourselves, we can change our thinking from negative, destructive thoughts to positive, empowering thoughts.

So how do you become more aware of when you're using destructive self-talk?

The way to become more aware of your positive or negative self-talk is by doing exactly what you are doing now: reading material that makes you more aware of what you are thinking.

I've been studying personal development for over 20 years and it's almost impossible for me to stay in a negative state of mind for long. Sure, I'm only human and still have negative thoughts, but I don't keep those thoughts for long because I know I am only hurting myself.

If I had never read a book on personal development and psychology, I can honestly say that I wouldn't have my high level of level of mental awareness or be as mentally tough as I am. This isn't because I'm brilliant; it's because I am so immersed in learning.

I've been fortunate enough to learn how to become tougher from some brilliant people in the world of psychology and personal development. And you can do exactly the same thing too. The more you read (from people who know what they're talking about), the more you will learn and the stronger you will become!

But this has to be a constant thing. The minute you take

your foot off the gas, your level of awareness and positivity will decrease. Some people think they can read one book or listen to one audiobook and that will change their life forever. There is no doubt that it will help you, but feeding yourself with positive information is just like taking a shower. You don't have one shower and say to yourself, "Well that's it now. I'm clean, so I never have to take another shower in my life."

You don't eat one healthy meal and think you'll be healthy for life.

It has to be a constant thing.

Reading personal development is like oxygen for your soul.

Whether it's reading my books or other authors' books.

There is nothing I can do in my life that you can't do with your life. You can achieve exceptional things in your life - and it all starts with your thinking!

CHAPTER 13

GET UP AND GET ON WITH IT

"It isn't the mountains ahead to climb that wear you out; it's the pebble in your shoe."
– Muhammad Ali

One day, I was playing football in the back garden with my son Léon. I soon found out he had a habit of falling over almost every time I went to tackle him. I didn't take his legs away from underneath him. In fact, I didn't even touch him, he just kept falling down.

I can only assume he picked that up from watching professional footballers to get a free-kick or a penalty. I was getting fed up with this and told him the next time he fell over I would stop playing football.

Miraculously, he stopped falling over.

So, what changed? Was it my style of football? Was I holding back from tackling him? Certainly not.

He was now:

1. Thinking about what he was doing.

2. Breaking his old habit because there was a reason for him to stay on his feet.

The funny thing is Léon is incredibly strong mentally. He did his first 10K when he was only eight years old and is the county running champion. When he goes for a run or he competes in a running event, he puts his big boy pants on and puts many of the adults to shame. When he was nine years old, he did a 5K Park Run competing against adult runners. He came 15th out of over 70 runners!

Léon didn't turn up and feel sorry for himself because he was only nine years old. He put his big boy pants on, ran his little heart out and kicked ass!

Many people have a learned helplessness that they pick up from others.

I'll never forget the time when I was working as a bouncer at one of my local pubs. A guy who was only in his 50s hobbled into the pub on his crutches. He went to the bar and had a few drinks, and after an hour or two he left.

However, when he left the pub, he left completely differently to when he first came in. He was walking without the support of his crutches and without a limp. It was as if he had gone to one of these evangelists and the evangelist had put his hand on the top of his head and said, "YOU ARE CURED, MY CHILD!"

As I witnessed this miraculous recovery several seconds later, the gentleman went back into his self-imposed disabled mode. Perhaps the alcohol in his system acted like a painkiller for a certain amount of time. I suppose you could also argue that he really had a disability. However, it is well known to those who know him that he puts on this act so he can claim benefits and not have to work for a living.

If somebody genuinely has disabilities, I'm all in favour of them getting support. And I'm more than happy that some of my taxes go to help people that need support.

I even spent several years as a support worker helping people with disabilities, epilepsy, autism and learning difficulties.

Many people get upset with others that claim benefits who don't deserve it. That's fine and I've got no argument with that, but I don't let these fakers upset me or ruin my day. I do, however, think about what they are missing out on in life with the facade they're putting on.

Most people don't have physical crutches, but many have mental crutches. They hold themselves back when they get up each morning and forget to put their big boy pants on. They put on frilly knickers and go into the world all precious and delicate like a little snowflake. It's almost like they wear a sign around their neck saying, "Please feel sorry for me."

That's not where you want to be in life. It's not who you are, at least I hope it's not. Chances are, if you started reading a book with the title, 'Put Your Big Boy Pants On,' you're made of stronger stuff than that.

People that want everybody to feel sorry for them are in the frilly knickers club, not the big boy pants club. This has nothing to do with gender. I know loads of women who are mentally stronger than many men I know.

Every morning we have to get up and put our big boy pants on. It's always important to think about the reason why you put on big boy pants. Is it to be a great mum or dad? Maybe it's reaching your next athletic goal? Is it to stay healthy? Putting on your big boy pants gets you infinitely more in life than putting on a set of frilly knickers.

The people who succeed and thrive in this world are the people who put their big boy pants on and get up and get on with it!

CHAPTER 14

LIES AND LAZINESS

"Truth matters. Don't take shortcuts, success doesn't count unless you earn it."

– Michelle Obama

I had a phone call from a friend on Facebook one evening.

He said he was with someone who was struggling with life and this guy recently nearly killed himself.

My friend said some people had called this guy a Walter Mitty – someone who bullshits and often makes up stories to make themselves look good. The guy had said that he had served with the SAS (Special Air Service). I told my friend to put this guy on the phone so I could talk to him. When he picked up the phone, I asked him what troop he was in when he served with the SAS.

He paused for a second and then said, "I was in red troop."

This was an immediate 'red flag' and from that point on, I knew he was lying.

If he had served in the SAS, he would've told me he was in either:

Mountain Troop
Mobility Troop
Boat Troop
or
Air Troop.

I asked them both what they had been doing that evening. My Facebook friend told me he had taken this guy out for a few drinks and they were now back at the guy's flat, knocking back more alcohol.

At the time I was in the middle of editing my book 'Man The F*ck Up' so my sympathy wasn't at its highest level.

I told him he needed to exercise, get around good people and lay off the drink.

My Facebook friend immediately jumped to the guy's defence and said, "He's been dry for 11 days now, but he had some bad news today, so we went out for a few drinks."

It was news about his benefits but I had little sympathy for him. If he had enough money to spend on alcohol, smoking cigarettes and doing whatever else he was doing, then why should I try to help him?

I told him he needed to man the fuck up and get a grip!

There was a moment of deathly silence on the other end of the phone. None of them expected me to say that. This guy was used to hearing the normal bullshit like, "It's going to be okay, you'll be fine."

The guy was used to people being nice to him. He expected some sympathy from me; however, that would've done him no good. This guy already had countless amounts of people feeling sympathetic and nice to him, and where did that get him? Absolutely nowhere!

Sometimes people will listen to endless hours of bullshit, but that's not how I roll.

When somebody is going through a challenging time, I'm not always blatantly rough with them, but I knew this guy had people mollycoddling him.

They were tiptoeing around him because he was always threatening to kill himself.

If somebody is in trouble, I'm more than happy to lend a sympathetic ear and help, but when someone lies to me straight away, I'm reluctant to hear their endless hours of bullshit. I've got no time for people that won't put the effort in to help themselves. I can't help them, and you can't help them unless they put their big boy pants on and help themselves!

In today's culture of cry-babies, words like this are deemed unacceptable to many.

If people aren't mollycoddled, they complain they are being unfairly treated.

It's easier for them to complain, stay in their negative mindset and get sympathy from everybody around them.

They love the attention they get from acting so hard done by; however, they will never live the good life if they keep acting that way.

If you're struggling with life, the bare minimum you can be with people is completely honest. When you're not honest with somebody who's trying to help you, then you are wasting their time and yours.

Have you ever tried to help someone like this?

If he had started off the phone call by being completely honest with who he was and what he had done, I would have been far more understanding.

The guy just needed to stop feeling sorry for himself, put his big boy pants on and get a grip!

Before writing these words, I was contacted by someone I used to take out running. He's a fantastic guy with a heart of gold but he bullshits quite a lot. When I started training him several years ago, I got into his car to head to a location for a run. While sitting in his passenger seat, I saw a two-litre bottle of Cola. I picked up the Cola, opened the car door, unscrewed the top and poured it onto the floor.

He looked at me with his mouth wide open in a state of pure shock and forcefully said,

"What the fuck are you doing?"

I told him I was pouring it away because of the amount of sugar in that two-litre bottle.

He wanted me to tell him he could keep on drinking sugary drinks, carry on eating his takeaway meals and train once or twice a week and that would make him lose weight and achieve his goals.

The last thing he wanted to hear was me saying,

"If you want to lose weight, you need to change some

things. Stop feeling sorry for yourself, change your habits, stop being a lazy fucker, and work your ass off!"

Harsh words? Maybe, but that's the reality of what it takes to achieve great things.

He didn't last long in his training and gave up. However, several years later he phoned me again and asked for my help.

I told him I would train him, and I didn't want any money, if he was serious about losing the weight.

"Yes, yes, I'm serious this time," he told me.

I arranged to meet him at a certain time at my house, but he never showed up. A week later he apologised for not turning up, made up a load of bullshit excuses and asked if he could see me again. I thought I'd give him another chance, so we arranged another time. Again, he didn't show up when he was supposed to.

Several months passed, and he messaged me again, asking me to help him lose weight.

"Can we train tonight?" he asked.

I told him I was tied up and couldn't do it at such short

notice; however, I told him we could train on Wednesday around 8pm and he agreed to show up.

But surprise, surprise, 8pm Wednesday came and went and there was no sign of him.

STRIKE 3!

Three days later I messaged him and told him,

"Hi mate, I won't be able to do any training with you in the future, I'm just too busy."

If somebody hasn't got the decency to let you help them when you're going out of your way for them, you have to move on. Of course, you don't have to move on. You can keep on spending time with time-wasters and destroy your own goals and dreams, but I wouldn't recommend it.

Laziness and lies kill dreams and outstanding achievements!

Also, notice he told me he wanted to train the very night he got back in touch with me. Sometimes people will do things on the spur of the moment. Maybe he watched a Rocky movie and was inspired. He may have listened to some music or read a book that inspired him in that moment.

It's fine being inspired for a moment because of an external source. My friend only wanted to train when he was inspired, but that's weak-ass thinking!

If you want to be a winner, you need to act towards your goals even when you don't want to sometimes. Achieving things isn't easy, and that's what separates the winners from the losers in life.

If you want to live the good life, there is no way around it. Be honest with people, accept help when you ask for it, put your big boy pants on and take action!

CHAPTER 15

CONSISTENCY IS KEY

"As long as you keep going, you'll keep getting better.
And as you get better, you gain more confidence.
That alone is success."
– Tamara Taylor

A few years ago, I interviewed an author called Michael Anderle.

Michael had become a tremendous success as a self-published author and was earning over $4 million a year within his first five years.

Several years later I was listening to Michael on a podcast. He said he believed he would lose 80% of his business if he stopped producing books.

When you haven't got momentum and you stop being active, you can lose not only your business or your job but also your health and fitness.

With fitness, I'm not a natural runner. The reason I got good at running was because I trained for an excessive number of hours compared to most people. If I take a long time off my training, my fitness goes downhill drastically and I become no fitter than the average person.

If I train one, two or three times a week, I become fit but nothing special. However, when I train 6 days a week, my fitness level goes through the roof!

If I hadn't run almost every day, I would never have broken the 100K Treadmill World Record, run 1,620 miles in America, or be placed first out of over 51,000 people in the 2014 and 2015 Strava Distance Challenge.

I know that if I only publish one book a year, the chances of my succeeding as an author are reduced. However, if I can publish 2, 4, 6 or more books a year, it gives me a much better chance of succeeding at the level I want to succeed.

When you're consistent, it can be tiring. However, if you want to succeed in a big way, put your big boy pants on and go the extra mile, even when you don't feel like it. That's the way it is. If you want to be above average or you want to be the absolute best, you have to work more than most people.

That's one reason the top people in their field succeed. They put more time and effort into their goal and they never give in. Of course, there are many keys to success which I write about in my books, but all successful people put their big boy pants on and work their ass off!

Sometimes you will put a lot of work in and you won't get the results that you want. You may think to yourself: I've done enough work now, I shouldn't have to do any more to reach my goals.

That's not the way life is. You have to put your big boy pants on every day to achieve your goals. When you take your foot off the gas, you're often not standing still, you're falling behind. You might not be the cleverest or the fastest, but when you are consistent, magical things will happen in your life.

It's like the story of the little steam engine that kept chugging away until it got to the top of the hill. Or like the tortoise and the hare. The tortoise relentlessly kept going and succeeded.

So, stay consistent, put the hours in and change your life for the better!

CHAPTER 16

YOU CAN TURN THINGS AROUND

"It's not how you start; it's how you finish."
– Serena Williams

When I wasn't the person I wanted to be, I didn't sit around for the next 5, 10 or 20 years thinking about why I wasn't better at this or that.

When I left school, I realised that if anyone was going to change my life, it was me. I had to put my big boy pants on, take responsibility for my life, and make the changes that needed to be changed.

No need to complain about my challenges because most of the time, nobody gives a shit. That's blunt, that's harsh, but that's also reality!

You have the power inside you to achieve great things in your life, but it all starts with you and your thinking. One day, I took my son Léon to the local market where there was a Christmas fayre on. It was there I saw an old school friend. We started talking and she asked me what was happening in my life.

I told her the main thing I concentrated on was spending quality time with Léon. I also told her about the exciting things happening within my author career and hosting and producing speaking events around the U.K. She stared at me, shook her head, and said, "Whatever happened to that boy I was in school with?"

She was referring to the person who I used to be and was comparing it to the person I have become.

I told her that the little boy I was had gone. In some ways I'm still the same person, but in some ways I'm not. Today I'm a lot more ambitious, driven and more focused than I was back then.

She was surprised at the person I have become because in school I was nothing special. If anything, I was below average with much of my schoolwork. In school, I never applied myself. I often got thrown out of class for talking and laughing. And that was when I could be bothered to turn up for class.

In school, you often learn subjects that are of no use to you later in life or subjects you have no interest in.

However, there are many brilliant things about school, and I would rather my son go to school than not be in school. In school he can learn to read and write and pick up a few other little skills along the way.

Lots of people think that if they haven't done well in school, they will not do well in life, which isn't true. I've studied the lives of many successful people and the facts are, even if you didn't do well in school, you can still achieve great things in your life.

It starts with a dream and the decision that you're going to go for your goals, but your dreams must be backed up with massive, focused action!

Too many people focus on the past and they let their past impede creating a better future for themselves. Even if you've achieved little in the past, you can still turn things around when the odds are against you!

Maybe you want to turn things around financially and physically. I know you can achieve that because I've done it with my own life. I've gone from being very unfit to fit. And I've gone from signing on the dole and getting paid £73 a week to earning more in one day than many people get paid in several months. And if I can do it, so can you.

Never, never lose hope. No matter what your circumstances are, you can change things for the better.

So put your big boy pants on, take massive action towards your goals and live the amazing life that you deserve to live!

ACKNOWLEDGEMENTS

It's almost impossible to say how many people have helped me along the way with producing this book, and if you're not in the acknowledgements just know that I am very grateful for your support and help.

However, I would like to say a massive THANK YOU to a few people that I can think of, off the top of my head:

Tracy and Kay Morris, Tom Webb, Paul 'The Viking' Hughes, Thomas Hughes, Eva Savage, Mark 'Billy' Billingham, Julie Colombino-Billingham, Cheryl Hicks, Jamie Baulch, Gene Hipgrave, Mark Dawson, Craig Martelle, Michael Anderle, James Blatch, Michael and Emma Byrne, Paul 'Faz' Farrington, Paul Heaney, James Atkinson, Des Powell and Laura Taylor.

Big thanks to 29 Commando Regiment, Royal Artillery, 3 Commando Brigade and The British Army.

Also, a huge THANKS to 'The Mark Llewhellin Advance Reader Team' for taking the time to read the manuscript and make suggestions.

ABOUT THE AUTHOR

In 1990, Mark Llewhellin left school without knowing his grades. He had little confidence and was not at all optimistic about his future.

Not knowing what to do with his life Mark followed some of his friends into the Army. He failed his basic 1.5-mile run, was bullied, and was also voted the fattest person in the Troop!

After a year with the Junior Leaders Regiment Royal Artillery, Mark decided he would try and get into 29 Commando Regiment Royal Artillery, which is an elite Army Commando Regiment that at the time proudly held the Military Marathon World Record (i.e. a marathon carrying a 40lbs backpack).

After failing the 29 Commando Selection phase (called 'The Beat Up') twice, first through lack of fitness and secondly through an injury, Mark subsequently passed on his third attempt and completed the 'All Arms Commando Course' on his first attempt.

Mark later went on to achieve the following:

- Break the 100-kilometre Treadmill World Record.
- Place 1st in the Strava Distance Challenge in 2015 competing against over 51,000 runners.
- Place 1st in the Strava Distance Challenge in 2014 competing against over 40,000 runners.
- Run and walk 70-miles without training on his 40th birthday.
- Become a successful Personal Fitness Trainer.
- Complete the Marathon Des Sables (a six-day, 135-mile ultra-marathon in the Sahara Desert).
- Work and live in London's exclusive Park Lane as a Bodyguard.

- Run 1,620 miles in the United States whilst carrying a 35lbs pack.

Mark has interviewed some of the world's top performers and high achievers in various locations, including one of the world's most prestigious memorabilia rooms…the Hard Rock Café Vault Room in London.

He has travelled to over 50 countries and has been featured in leading national newspapers and on TV for his running achievements.

Mark has extensively worked in the support and care industry for many years helping individuals with brain injury, autism, epilepsy, dyspraxia, and various types of learning difficulties.

He is the Managing Director of Mark 7 Productions, as well as the Producer and Host of 'An Audience with Mark Billy Billingham' speaking events around the UK.

Mark is currently working on more personal development books and lives with his son Léon (when Léon's not at his Mum's) on a beautiful marina in South West Wales.

ALSO BY MARK LLEWHELLIN

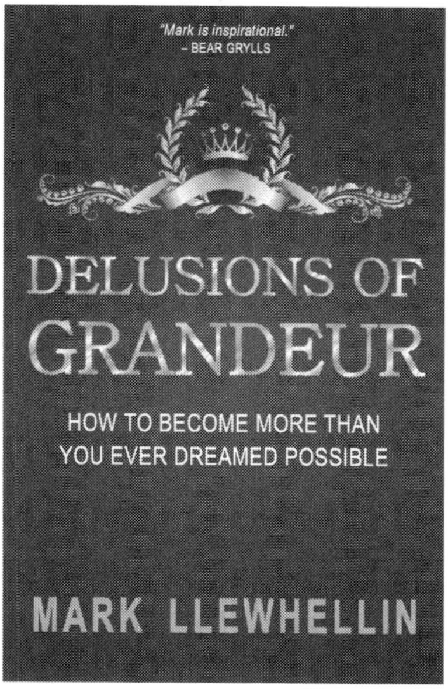

"Powerful. A must read!"
Mark 'Billy' Billingham – TV's Most Highly Decorated SAS Leader
MAN THE F*CK UP
HOW TO PICK YOURSELF UP AND SUCCEED WHEN LIFE BITCH SLAPS YOU
MARK LLEWHELLIN

NUMBER 1 BESTSELLING AUTHOR
SMUG BASTARD
DEVELOP UNSTOPPABLE SELF CONFIDENCE
AND GO SCREAMING PAST PEOPLE THAT HATE YOUR GUTS
MARK LLEWHELLIN

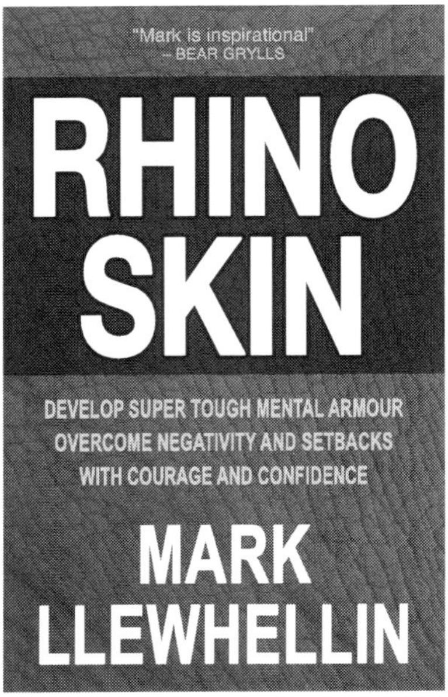
"Mark is inspirational"
– BEAR GRYLLS
RHINO SKIN
DEVELOP SUPER TOUGH MENTAL ARMOUR OVERCOME NEGATIVITY AND SETBACKS WITH COURAGE AND CONFIDENCE
MARK LLEWHELLIN

NUMBER 1 BESTSELLING AUTHOR
STAY STRONG
ELIMINATE NEGATIVE THINKING AND BECOME A STRONGER AND MORE POSITIVE PERSON
MARK LLEWHELLIN

NUMBER 1 BESTSELLING AUTHOR
SMALL CHANGES
REMARKABLE RESULTS
TIME TO
TOUGHEN
UP
DEVELOP IMMENSE INNER STRENGTH AND CONFIDENCE
OVERCOME CHALLENGES AND ACHIEVE YOUR GOALS
MARK
LLEWHELLIN

JUST
NUMBER 1 BESTSELLING AUTHOR
MARK LLEWHELLIN
KEEP
THE POWER OF POSITIVE THINKING
PATIENCE AND PERSISTENCE
GOING

AN EASY GUIDE TO ACHIEVING YOUR GOALS
AND TRANSFORMING YOUR LIFE
JUST GO
FOR IT
NUMBER 1 BESTSELLING AUTHOR
MARK
LLEWHELLIN
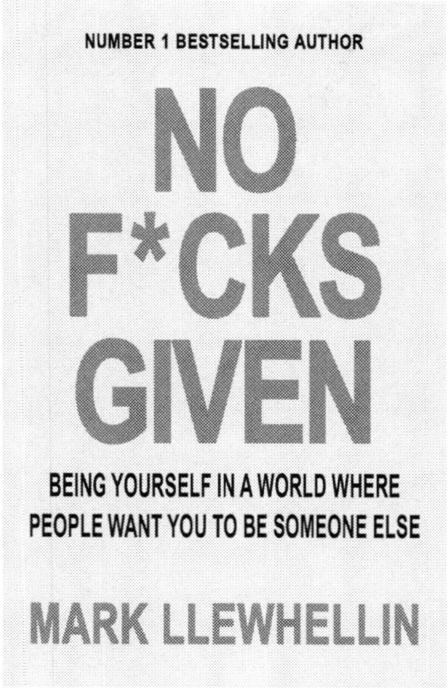
NUMBER 1 BESTSELLING AUTHOR
NO
F*CKS
GIVEN
BEING YOURSELF IN A WORLD WHERE
PEOPLE WANT YOU TO BE SOMEONE ELSE
MARK LLEWHELLIN

GET TWO FREE MARK LLEWHELLIN BOOKS AND DEALS AND UPDATES

Join 'The Mark Llewhellin Advance Reader Team' for information on new books and deals plus:

You can pick up FREE copies of Mark's five star reviewed books:

1. 'The Underdog'

2. 'Delusions of Grandeur'

Simply go to Mark's website at www.markllewhellin.com and sign up for FREE.

REFERENCES

Constructing the tallest building in the world – Burj Khalifa documentary. Official HD Documentary.

Big Bigger Biggest

National Geographic – Megastructures

The Legendary Honey Badger – National Geographic

African environmental films – The Meanest Animal in the World

Inventor of the Disposable Culture: King Camp Gillette

Discovery World

Evan Carmichael

Smithsonian Channel

Wikipedia

Business Insider

Ranker

Forbes

DISCLAIMER

A Mark 7 Publications Paperback.

First published in Great Britain in 2021

by Mark 7 Publications

ISBN 978-1-914006-53-1

Book design and formatting by Tom Webb
pixelfiddler@hotmail.co.uk

IF YOU ENJOYED THIS BOOK

Your help in spreading the word about Mark's books is greatly appreciated and your reviews make a huge difference to help new readers change their lives for the better.

If you found this book useful please leave a review on the platform you purchased it on.

Live Your Dreams!

Mark

Printed in Great Britain
by Amazon

66048282R00097

Life and work in a MIDDLESEX VILLAGE: Harefield 1880 – 1914

Geoffrey Tyack

HILLINGDON BOROUGH LIBRARIES
1984

ISBN 0 907869 05 X
Designed by the London Borough of
Hillingdon Publicity Section
and printed by Echo Press (1983) Ltd., Loughborough
for Hillingdon Borough Libraries,
High Street, Uxbridge, Middlesex.